FOOD AND CELEBRATIONS
FRANCE

Sylvia Goulding

WAYLAND

First published in 2008 by Wayland
(a division of Hachette Children's Books)
First published in paperback in 2012 by Wayland

Wayland
Hachette Children's Books
338 Euston Road
London NW1 3BH

Wayland Australia
Level 17/207 Kent Street
Sydney NSW 2000

© 2008 Brown Bear Books Ltd

Brown Bear Books Ltd
First Floor
9–17 St. Albans Place
London N1 0NX

All rights reserved. This book is protected by copyright.
No part of it may be reproduced, stored in a retrieval
system, or transmitted in any form or by any means,
without the prior permission in writing of the Publisher,
nor be otherwise circulated in any form of binding or
cover other than that in which it is published and
without a similar condition including this condition
being imposed on the subsequent publisher.

ISBN: 978-0-7502-6939-1

Printed in China

Wayland is a division of Hachette Children's Books,
an Hachette UK Company.
www.hachette.co.uk

10 9 8 7 6 5 4 3 2 1

Photographic Credits:
Front and Back Cover: Klaus Arras
Pierre-Jérôme Atger: 31; **Fotolia:** 6; **Mike Goulding:**
13, 20, 22, 37, 38; **iStock:** title page, 3, 4, 14, 30, 35, 39;
Nathalie Le Marrec: 28; **Shutterstock:** 5, 7, 8, 9, 10,
12, 13, 21, 23, 24, 29, 30, 36

With thanks to models:
Caspar, Ella, Eugene, Felix, Jeremy, Phoebe

Cooking Editor
Angelika Ilies has always been interested in cookery
and other countries. She studied nutritional sciences
in college. She has lived in the United States, England
and Germany. She has also traveled extensively and
collected international recipes on her journeys.
Angelika has written more than 70 cookbooks and
cooking card series. She currently lives in Frankfurt,
Germany, with her two children and has spent much
time researching children's nutrition. Both children
regularly cook with their mother.

Project Editor: Sylvia Goulding
Cooking Editor: Angelika Ilies
Contributors: Jacqueline Fortey, Sylvia Goulding
Photographers: Klaus Arras, Emanuelle Morgan
Cartographer: Darren Awuah
Art Editor: Paula Keogh
Illustrator: Jo Gracie
Picture Researcher: Mike Goulding
Managing Editor: Bridget Giles
Production Director: Alastair Gourlay
Editorial Director: Lindsey Lowe
Children's Publisher: Anne O'Daly

To be carried out safely, many of the recipes in this book
require adult supervision and assistance. While rules and safety
precautions have been noted throughout the book, readers are
reminded always to use caution when cooking, using sharp tools,
or lighting fires. The publisher, editors and authors have made
every reasonable effort to ensure that the recipes in this book are
safe when followed as instructed but assume no responsibility for
any damage caused or sustained while carrying out the recipes in
the book. The recipes and ingredients recommended for the dishes
contained in this book are aimed at healthy individuals and are
not specific to any individuals or their particular circumstances.
Always check the list of ingredients for each specific dish. If you
are in any doubt as to whether an ingredient is inappropriate for
you, you should consult your GP. Do not use any ingredients that
you may be allergic to (or think you may have an allergy to).

Contents

KT-226-020

let's START COOKING

Cooking is fun – you learn about different ingredients and cooking methods, you find out how things taste, and you can serve a meal to your family and friends that you have cooked yourself! Some of the recipes in this book have steps that need adult help – ask a parent or other adult if they will be your kitchen assistant while you cook a meal.

This line tells you how many people the meal will feed.

In this box, you find out which ingredients you need for your meal.

WHAT YOU NEED:

SERVES 4 PEOPLE:

500g white rice
4 eggs, beaten
light soy sauce
4 tablespoons
   groundnut oil
2 onions
50g peeled prawns
50g ham
50g peas

Check before you start that you have everything you need. Get all the ingredients ready before you start cooking.

◁ Fresh fruits or vegetables are ripe when they have a strong aroma. Whenever I can, I like to feel and smell fruit or vegetables before I buy them.

! WHEN TO GET help

Most cooking involves cutting ingredients and heating them in some way, whether frying, boiling or cooking in the oven. Each time you see this exclamation mark, be extra careful as you cook and make sure your adult kitchen assistant is around to help.

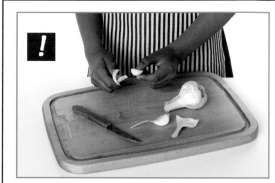

For many meals you need to chop an onion. First cut off a thin slice at both ends. Pull off the peel. Cut the onion in half from end to end. Put one half with the cut side down on the chopping board. Hold it with one hand and cut end-to-end slices with the other hand. Hold the slices together and cut across the slices to make small cubes. Make sure you do not cut yourself!

Other recipes in this book use fresh garlic. Break a whole head of garlic into separate cloves. Cut the top and the bottom off each clove, and pull off the papery skin. Now you can either chop the garlic clove with a sharp knife, or you can use a garlic crusher to squeeze the garlic directly into the frying pan or saucepan. If you are worried about garlic breath, chew some parsley.

A **barbecue** is not essential, but in the summer French people often like to cook a meal outdoors.

With a **garlic crusher** you can crush garlic into a purée for sauces, when you do not want to add garlic pieces.

Oil and vinegar, together with garlic, mustard, salt and pepper, make a typical French salad dressing called *vinaigrette*.

A flameproof casserole dish is used for making stews and roasts. It has a tight-fitting lid.

A trip around
FRANCE

France is the largest country in western Europe and is about five times as big as the UK. It is famed for its beautiful countryside, rich culture and delicious food.

France is nicknamed the 'hexagon' because it fits into a six-sided shape. An ocean and a sea form three of its sides. The coastline has rugged cliffs, windswept dunes, sandy beaches and rocky coves. In the south, the coast meets the warm Mediterranean Sea. The narrow English Channel separates northern France from England.

Belgium and Luxembourg are France's northern neighbours. Germany and Switzerland are on the east side, and Italy is to the south-east. France's south-western border with Spain runs through the Pyrenees mountain range.

France has mostly fairly cool winters and mild summers. But the south is much warmer and the east much colder than the rest of the country.

The north

The north-western regions of Normandy and Brittany have lovely beaches, cliffs, bays and harbours. Wide, flat plains and gentle hills stretch across much of northern France. They form an area around the River Seine called the Paris Basin.

◁ **More than 63 million people** live in France. Its main immigrant groups consist of southern and eastern Europeans, North Africans and Arabs.

NORTH
AMERICA

ASIA

EUROPE

—FRANCE

AFRICA

ATLANTIC OCEAN

◁ **France** is a country in western Europe. It borders Spain, Belgium, Luxembourg, Germany, Switzerland and Italy.

▽ **Paris** is the capital of France. It lies on the River Seine in northern France. The Eiffel Tower is one of its famous landmarks.

ENGLAND

NETHERLANDS

ENGLISH CHANNEL

BELGIUM

Lille

LUXEMBOURG

GERMANY

1

2

NORMANDY

Seine

ARDENNES

1

BRITTANY

PARIS

Strasbourg

2

Loire

Orléans

Loire

4

FRANCE

SWITZERLAND

△ **Mont-St-Michel** is a rocky island off the Normandy coast. A causeway links it to the mainland.

Bordeaux

Lyon

Garonne

AUVERGNE

4

Rhône

△ **The Massif Central** and the Auvergne region in southern central France were once volcanic. They have spectacular river gorges, spa towns and rugged cliffs and craters.

AQUITAINE

PYRENEES

Toulouse

PROVENCE

3

SPAIN

Marseilles

MEDITERRANEAN SEA

CORSICA

ITALY

◁ **Provence** is a large region in south-eastern France. It is famous for its purple lavender fields and for its herbs. *Herbes de Provence* is a mixture that includes rosemary, thyme, bay leaf and marjoram.

SARDINIA

3

Near the country's north and eastern borders, the landscape changes. The Ardennes region is part of a forest plateau with ridges and deep valleys. Farther east, the Vosges mountains stretch along the west bank of the River Rhine.

Central France

Two famous wine-growing regions lie south of the Paris Basin. The rich province of Burgundy to the east stretches down to the large city of Lyon. To the west, the Loire Valley is known for its wine and splendid castles.

Below these regions lies the Massif Central. This huge plateau makes up nearly one-fifth of France's total area. The area has a dramatic landscape that was created by volcanic eruptions long ago. It is the source of several rivers, including the Dordogne, the Loire, the Lot and the Tarn. The Tarn and the Aveyron rivers have worn away limestone rocks to form deep gorges. They attract rock climbers, hikers and white-water rafters.

Farther east, the River Rhône flows from north to south through a wide valley. Beyond the river to the east are the snowy peaks of the French Alps. Here is Europe's highest mountain, Mont Blanc (4,810 metres).

Southern France

The River Garonne flows north-west from the Pyrenees into the huge estuary (river mouth) at Bordeaux. This trading port is at the centre of a world-famous region for wine. Vast sand dunes stretch southwards along the Atlantic coast. This area contains huge pine trees, ponds, marshes and moors. The countryside in Poitou and Aquitaine is fairly flat until it

▽ *Château de Chambord* is the largest of the magnificent castles in the Loire Valley. The château is 128 metres long. It has 440 rooms, 365 fireplaces, 13 staircases and stables for 1,200 horses. It stands in a park that is surrounded by a 35-km-long wall.

reaches the craggy peaks of the Pyrenees. This mountain range runs across south-west France almost to the Mediterranean. Bears and mountain goats live here.

Sunny Provence in the south-east has many resorts. Flamingoes wade and white horses roam in the salt marshes of the Camargue, west of Marseille. In the east, the land rises sharply into the Alpes-Maritimes. These mountains run along the beautiful Côte d'Azur (Azure Coast).

▽ **The town of Luzech** in the south-west stands in one of many loops made by the River Lot. The river meanders (follows a winding and turning course) past hilltops planted with vines.

ALL SORTS OF CHÂTEAUX

France has about 40,000 castles, or châteaux. Some are magnificent and huge, but some look just like simple farmhouses. Any building on a wine estate can call itself a château – whether it has lots of turrets or not!

The food we grow in
FRANCE

France is the most important farming country in western Europe. About two-thirds of the country is farmland.

*T*he largest French farms are on the northern plains and in the west. Near Calais, people grow potatoes and sugarbeet. The Paris Basin has very fertile soil. Here, farmers grow wheat, barley, corn and peas. In Normandy, on the north-west coast, herds of cows graze in the fields. Their milk is made into cream, cheese and butter. Lamb is raised on salt marshes near the coast, and apples are grown to make into cider.

The landscape in Champagne is covered with vines growing grapes for sparkling wine. There are also vineyards in Alsace-Lorraine, around the Vosges mountains. People here grow hops, which are used for brewing beer. Local specialities are hams, soft cheese, sauerkraut (pickled cabbage) and cakes. The orchards and market gardens are filled with cherry trees, blueberry bushes and raspberry canes.

Central France

The rocky regions of the Massif Central in the south are too bleak to grow many crops. But the Loire Valley is sometimes called the 'Garden of France', because fruit and vegetables thrive

△ *Cows in Normandy* yield the milk to make the world-famous French soft cheeses brie, camembert and Pont l'Évêque. Other great dairy products from this region are the cream and butter from the town of Isigny.

in its rich soil. A meal in a local restaurant might include freshwater fish followed by cheese and *tarte tatin* (apple tart). Caves alongside the River Loire are cool and dark – perfect for growing mushrooms.

In the Rhône Valley, peaches, apricots, plums and tomatoes are grown on small farms. The beautiful region of Burgundy is famous for its great wines and hearty beef stews. The town of Bresse advertises its produce with a giant metal chicken by the side of the road – chickens here are supposed to be the tastiest in the world.

Dijon is the home of a strong mustard. It was once made from seed grown in the fields around Dijon, but now most mustard seed is imported from Canada. The city of Lyon is known as a centre for food lovers.

There are lush green meadows in the Franche-Comté region, along the Swiss border. Here cowbells chime as brown and white cows munch the grass. Cheese makers mature large drums of nutty Comté cheese from their milk. This cheese is good for melting in soups, gratins and other baked dishes. In the mountains, people make smoked sausages and hams.

A CHEESE A DAY

French people make about 400 different cheeses. That's more than one different cheese for every single day of the year!

South-western France

In the south-west, the local produce includes many duck and goose products, such as pâtés, goose gizzards (second stomach) and duck breasts. Both birds are preserved in their own fat; this is called *confit*. Goose fat is also used to cook many dishes.

In the Périgord and Quercy regions, rare strong-smelling fungi called truffles grow under trees, particularly oaks. Nuts from walnut groves are used to make walnut oil. Fields of sunflowers are also grown to make oil.

Aquitaine, with its Atlantic coastline, has dairy farms, fruit orchards and market gardens. The Basque capital, Bayonne, is famous for its hams. In Languedoc-Roussillon, market gardeners grow delicious pitted fruits, such as peaches and apricots.

South-eastern France

Farmers keep sheep on the wetlands of the Camargue. The scent of herbs and lavender is in the air in neighbouring Provence. Farmers also grow garlic, peppers, tomatoes, aubergines, olives and fennel. These ingredients appear in local dishes, such as a vegetable stew called *ratatouille*, in *salade Niçoise*, and in *aïoli*, vegetables with a garlic mayonnaise.

Fishing

France is one of the largest fishing nations in the European Union. Small boats fish in the waters around Brittany and along the Mediterranean coast. Larger boats set sail for longer trips from ports such as Concarneau in Brittany, and Boulogne in the north. Shellfish, especially oysters, scallops and clams, are farmed and collected in the bays of Brittany. The Bassin d'Arcachon south of Bordeaux is another area where oysters are farmed. In Provence, a fish stew called *bouillabaisse* is a speciality.

◁ *Geese and ducks* are raised in south-western France. They are roasted, preserved in their own fat, cured or smoked like hams, made into pâté and sausages, or stewed in wine. Often they are served with fruits – orange, prunes or grapefruit.

▽ **Fishing boats** lie anchored in a harbour in Corsica. Fishers catch sea urchins, which are eaten raw, gold bream, St Pierre-fish and red barbel. Fish are often served grilled. Delicacies include perch and lobster.

RURAL FRANCE

While most French people live in towns, the countryside is still a lively place. Even if people work in an office, they often have some land.

People grow fruit and vegetables in their gardens, and they may also keep a few chickens and some sheep.

let's make...
ALSACE ONION TART

This savoury open tart comes from the Alsace region in eastern France. Grandma used the onions from her own garden to make it, and she always served it hot.

WHAT YOU NEED:

MAKES 6 PORTIONS:

225g plain flour
½ teaspoon salt

1 egg
340g cold butter

FOR THE TOPPING:

575g onions
25g butter
salt, black pepper
paprika
2 tablespoons flour

1 cup milk
2 egg yolks
240ml double cream
125g lean smoked ham
125g Gruyère cheese

PLUS:

1 quiche dish, 250mm wide

◁ This tart makes a nice light lunch or supper. We eat it with a simple green salad, some crusty bread and a glass of juice.

EASY onion tart

Instead of making the dough yourself, you could also use ready-made pastry. Choose a puff pastry for a change, or try making this tart with a pizza base. For the topping, you could add some chopped fresh parsley, or use a cream cheese instead of the milk and double cream.

1 Knead together the ingredients for the dough. Shape it into a ball and wrap it in cling filml. Chill for about 1 hour. Meanwhile peel the onions and cut them into very thin slices. Separate the slices into rings.

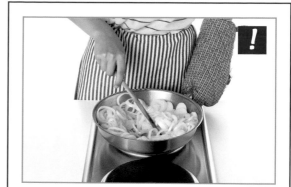

2 Melt half the butter in a saucepan. Add the onion rings and fry and stir for 3 minutes, until they are golden. Season with salt, pepper and paprika.

3 Melt the rest of the butter in a second saucepan. Tip in the flour, stir and fry until it is golden. Continue stirring, while you add the milk, a little at a time. Cook over a low heat for about 5 minutes. Take the saucepan off the heat. Stir in the egg yolks and the cream, and then the onions.

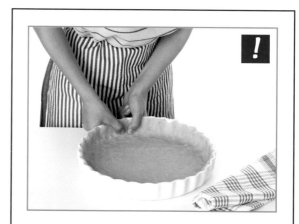

4 Heat the oven to 200°C (gas mark 6). Knead the dough again, then roll it out thinly. Line the quiche dish with the dough. Cut off the overlap.

5 Spread the onion mixture on to the dough. Chop the ham into cubes and grate the cheese. Sprinkle the tart with both. Bake in the oven for 40 minutes. Allow the tart to rest for 10 minutes before cutting.

let's make...
POTATO GRATIN

Gratin dauphinois (say 'gra-taing dau-fee-nwah') is a speciality from Grenoble, in the foothills of the Alps. These scalloped potatoes are cooked until they are golden and crusty.

WHAT YOU NEED:

SERVES 3-4 PEOPLE:

450g waxy potatoes, for
   example Desirée
2 garlic cloves
2 tablespoons butter
   (plus some more to grease
   the kitchen foil)
3 eggs
400ml whipping cream
   or milk
salt, white pepper

◁ Potato gratin is a perfect winter dish. It's great on its own or with sausages. My mum cooks this dish on a Monday, and serves it with the leftovers from the Sunday roast.

WHAT'S THIS: gratin?

Almost any vegetable can be made into a gratin – a dish with cream or cheese that is cooked in the oven to get a crust. Potatoes are often included.

MY TIP

Choose potatoes that are about the same size and shape so they all cook evenly.

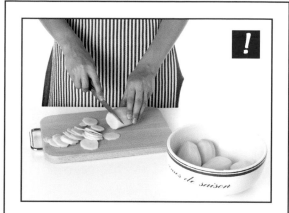

1 Heat the oven to 200°C (gas mark 6). Peel the potatoes, wash them and cut them into thin slices.

2 Peel and finely chop the onion *(see page 5)*. Melt the butter in a frying pan until it foams. Add the onion and fry it until it is transparent (see-through). Empty the frying pan into a gratin dish. Spread the onion and butter around in the dish to grease it. **!**

3 Arrange the potato slices in the dish in overlapping circles.

4 In a bowl, whisk together the eggs with the cream or milk. Season with plenty of salt and pepper. Pour the mixture over the potatoes.

5 Grease a sheet of kitchen foil with butter, then use it to cover the dish. Bake the potatoes for about 20 minutes. **!**

6 Take off the foil and bake the gratin for 30 to 40 minutes more, until the potatoes start to look golden brown. Check that the potatoes are done – if you stick in a sharp knife they should feel just about soft. **!**

let's make...
SALADE NIÇOISE

A basket of sun-ripened vegetables goes into this salad from the town of Nice, in southern France. Nice is nice, but it's pronounced 'nees' and the salad is a 'salard nee-swahrze'.

WHAT YOU NEED:

SERVES 4 PEOPLE:

225g small potatoes
250g green beans
salt, black pepper
1 onion
4 tomatoes
 1 small green pepper
  ½ cucumber

1 tin tuna in spring
 water (150g)
½ lettuce
10 black olives
4 sprigs basil

FOR THE DRESSING:

4 tablespoons red wine
 vinegar
1 garlic clove
1 teaspoon mustard
6 tablespoons
 olive oil

◁ I bought all the ingredients for this salad in the market. Now I'll make this refreshing lunch.

MY TIP

Try adding some hard-boiled eggs. Boil the eggs in their shells in hot water for about 8 minutes. Refresh them under cold water, shell them when they're cold enough to touch, then cut each egg into quarters and add.

1 Wash the potatoes and boil them in their skins in a little water for about 15–20 minutes until they are only just soft. Drain and allow to cool, then peel and slice the potatoes.

3 Peel and halve the onion, then cut it into thin half-moons. Separate these. Wash the tomatoes and cut them into eighths. Remove the stem ends. Wash, trim, halve and de-seed the pepper, then cut it into strips.

2 Wash and trim the beans. Cook them in salted water for 10 minutes over a low heat. Drain, then rinse them under cold water. Drain in a sieve.

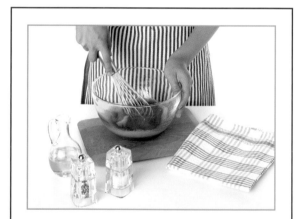

4 Peel the cucumber and halve it lengthways. Cut into half-moons. Drain the tuna. Wash the lettuce, shake it dry, and tear it into smaller pieces.

5 In a bowl, combine the vinegar and mustard. Press in the garlic. Whisk in the olive oil, a little at a time, until you have a creamy dressing.

6 Put all the vegetables into the bowl and turn them with spoons until they are coated all over. Sprinkle in the olives and some basil leaves.

How we celebrate in
FRANCE

People in France enjoy eleven national holidays. Most are celebrated with big meals, dances and fireworks.

French holidays celebrate important days in the country's history, such as the French Revolution in 1789, Armistice (peace) after World War I in 1918 and Victory (from German rule) after World War II in 1945. Other French holidays are Christian celebrations, including Easter, Whitsun and Christmas.

Bastille Day

Bastille Day is the French National Holiday, or la Fête Nationale. It is also known by its date, *Quatorze Juillet* – 14 July. Bastille Day is a bit like Independence Day in the United States. The festival remembers the events of 14 July 1789. On that day, people stormed the Bastille prison in Paris. They were protesting against the rule of a corrupt king and queen. Their protest was the start of the French Revolution.

> ▷ **Honorary citizens** sport the national flag for a ceremony in a small town on Bastille Day, 14 July. A band plays the national anthem, which is known as the Marseillaise. Sometimes a recording of the anthem is played. Then people shout: 'Vive la France!' and continue with the festivities.

▷ **Spectacular fireworks** are part of most celebrations in France. There are always huge fireworks for Bastille Day on 14 July, but you can also enjoy fireworks during every village fête. Many people also buy fireworks to celebrate a birthday or other family occasion.

Nowadays, the event is marked by a military parade in Paris. The president leads the parade. Jets fly overhead in formation, blazing the national colours: blue, white and red. In smaller towns, there are similar ceremonies, often at war memorials. During the day, there are fairs and fun events all over France. At night, people enjoy large feasts and dance until the fireworks at midnight.

MUSIC FOR FREE

21 June is the Fête de la Musique. All over France, musicians play for free in the streets. You can hear rock, reggae, country, techno, rap, classical and also traditional French songs, or chansons.

Le Tour

The Tour de France is a huge cycle race around France. It takes three weeks to complete. Often the Tour also visits neighbouring countries, such as Belgium or England across the Channel. While the cycle race is not a national holiday, many people are given the day off by their employers when the race passes through their town or village.

People line the roads and find the best spot to stand hours before the Tour passes. This is because the 'Caravane' arrives before the cyclists. The Caravane is a publicity convoy of about 300 cars. They advertise anything from savings banks to mobile phones, and throw some ten million samples or gifts, such as keyrings, to the spectators. After the Caravane has gone, the cyclists and their support vehicles pass, and then everyone has a barbecue or a party.

▽ **The 'Caravane'** is a convoy of advertising cars or floats that runs for about one hour before the cyclists in the Tour de France.

Toussaint

Toussaint is All Saints' Day, on 1 November. This Catholic holiday celebrates all the saints who do not have their own saint's day at one time. It is also a day to remember the departed; people clean and decorate the graves of their dead. Today, typical Halloween customs are also celebrated in France. French children trick-or-treat, carve jack-o'-lanterns, and dress up in scary costumes.

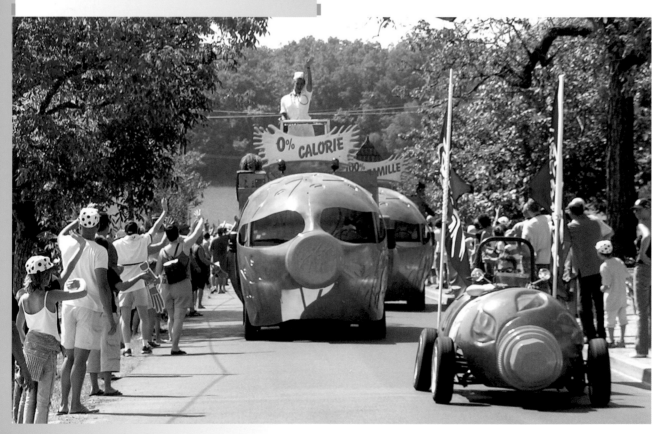

Lyon Festival of Light

This religious festival was first celebrated in 1852. The faithful of Lyon wanted to set up a statue of the Virgin Mary on top of a hill. They had already delayed this event because of floods. On 8 December, everyone lit candles in their homes to celebrate, but a terrible storm threatened. The storm passed quickly, and the citizens lit up their homes and the streets. They danced and celebrated. They still do this today.

△ **The Festival of Light** in Lyon, southern France, now lasts for the four days nearest each 8 December. Spectacular light displays bathe the city's monuments, squares and public buildings in glorious colours.

let's make...
MÉCHOUI

This dish (pronounced 'mayshwee') came to France from North Africa. At village fêtes, we roast one or several whole lambs on a spit, but here is our family-sized version.

WHAT YOU NEED:

SERVES 4-6 PEOPLE:

1 small leg of lamb
(weighing about 2.5–3kg)
a handful of fresh mint
leaves
4 garlic cloves
2 tablespoons paprika
3 teaspoons ground cumin
4 tablespoons sunflower
oil or butter
salt and ground
cumin for sprinkling

◁ The roast lamb is so tender you don't need a knife to cut it. You just pull off a piece and eat it with your fingers.

WHAT'S THIS: méchoui?

Méchoui means 'barbecued lamb'. In North Africa, the lamb is traditionally cooked over a hole in the ground. In France, large barbecue grills are often made from several half oil drums. These are filled with wood, including the prunings from vines. The lambs are roasted all day and served at the festive meal in the evening.

1 Wash the mint and shake it dry. Pull off the leaves and chop them very finely. Peel and press the garlic *(see page 5)*. In a large bowl, stir the mint, garlic, paprika, cumin and oil together to make a paste.

2 Put the meat in the bowl and rub the spice paste all over. Make sure every part of the lamb is coated. Place the meat in a roasting tin and cover it with a clean teatowel. Allow it to marinate for at least 1 hour.

3 Heat the oven to 190°C (gas mark 5). Cook the lamb for about 2–2½ hours, depending on its size.

4 The meat should be so tender that you can pull pieces off the roast with your fingers. But do not touch the meat until it has cooled a little. Sprinkle the roast with salt and cumin and serve.

let's make...
CRÊPES SUZETTE

Crêpes are sold at almost all fairgrounds, so whenever I think of festivals and holidays I think of crêpes Suzette. In restaurants, the crêpes are often flamed with alcohol.

WHAT YOU NEED:

MAKES 8 CRÊPES:

2 eggs
250ml milk
85g plain flour
1 tablespoon sugar
2 tablespoons unsalted
    butter

FOR THE SAUCE:

2 large untreated organic
    oranges
225g sugar

PLUS:

2 oranges
2½ tablespoons unsalted
    butter for baking

◁ One day I'd like
to be head waiter.
I would cook crêpes
Suzette and flame
the crêpes in front
of the guests.

WHAT'S THIS: crêpe?

A crêpe is a type of pancake. It is much thinner than a normal pancake. There are sweet and savoury crêpes. Often the savoury crêpes are made with wholemeal flour. Crêpes can be filled with all sorts of foods – sweet apples, berries, marmalade; or savoury ham, cheese and mushrooms. Crêpes are a specialty of Brittany in northern France.

1 Stir together the eggs, milk, flour and sugar to make a batter. Heat the butter in a small frying pan until it is golden brown and stir it into the mixture. Set the batter aside.

2 To make the sauce, scrub the oranges under hot water and pat them dry. With a potato peeler, pare off the zest of one orange in thin strips. Squeeze out the juice. In a saucepan, cook the zest, juice and sugar over a high heat to make a thin syrup.

3 Peel the remaining two oranges. Also completely peel off the white inner skins. With a sharp knife, cut out the orange slices between their thin skins. Catch the juice.

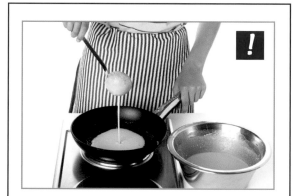

4 In two non-stick frying pans melt some of the butter until it foams. Pour in 1 ladleful of batter. Turn the frying pan so the batter covers the whole base. Fry the crêpe for 1 minute, then carefully turn it over with a wooden spatula. Now fry the other side for only about 30 seconds.

5 Place the finished crêpes on a rack and cover them with a clean teatowel. Fry six more crêpes as above.

6 Place the orange slices on the crêpes and fold the crêpes over. Put the crêpes back into the frying pan, pour over the syrup and heat through for 1 minute.

How we celebrate at home in
FRANCE

In France, people love their food. To celebrate a personal event, such as a birthday or a wedding, they will spare no money or effort to prepare a grand celebratory meal. Such meals are also a way of thanking friends and neighbours for their help during the harvest, for example picking grapes.

▽ *Family banquets* for special occasions such as weddings often take place in people's own homes. Long tables and benches are set out in the garden and covered with white tablecloths. Everyone joins in. The meals often last for many hours, and the dancing and the music carry on through the night.

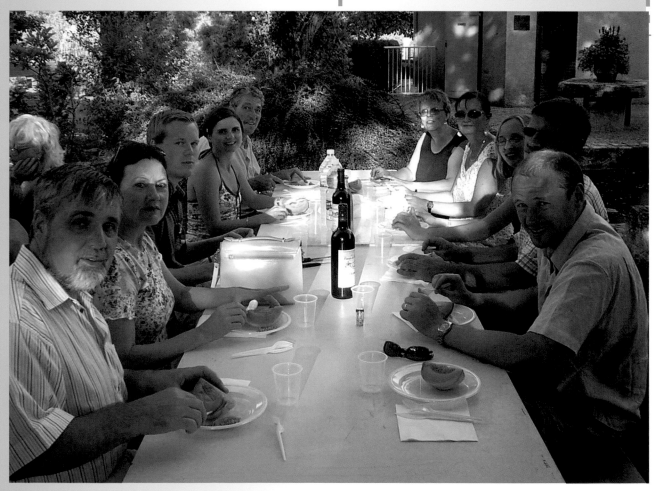

Festive meals

A traditional French meal has many courses. The meal starts with pre-dinner drinks called *aperitif* and savoury snacks or olives. Then people sit down and have the first course, which is often a soup, for example onion soup. After that they have a plate of ham, pâté and cold meats called *charcuterie*, melon or a seafood salad. This is followed by the *entrée*, a second course, often of fish. Afterwards there is the main meat course, for example duck breast, roast meat, a stew or a steak. The vegetables often follow separately, after the meat. Then there will be a green salad, to give a fresh taste. Finally, a plate of different cheeses is followed by dessert. *Bon appetit!*

Christmas

Families celebrate Christmas together with a late and very festive meal on Christmas Eve. Many homes have a Christmas tree and a crèche (model of the Nativity scene). Santa Claus is known in France as Père Noël. He arrives late at night, when young children are already asleep. Père Noël leaves the gifts next to the tree, in shoes, or in Christmas stockings. Religious people go to midnight mass. The churches are beautifully lit and the bells ring out Christmas carols.

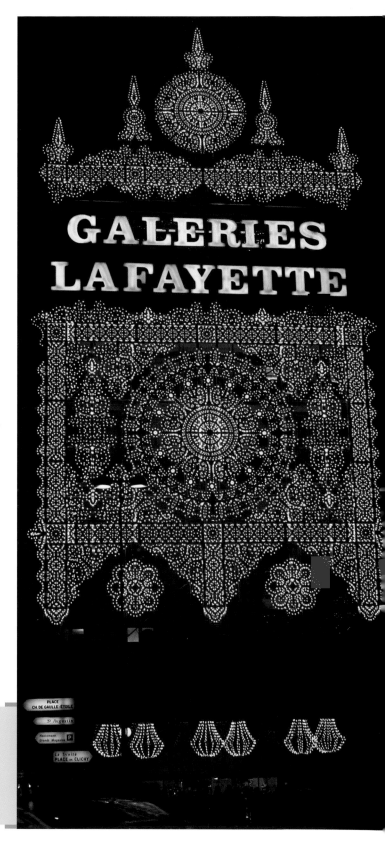

▷ **Christmas decorations** can be seen on most shops, as in this famous department store in Paris. But aside from having a real Christmas tree with candles, people do not normally decorate their homes for Christmas.

◁ *Lilies of-the-valley* are the flowers that people give each other on 1 May, as a token of happiness. Many flowers link to special days: on 1 November, chrysanthemums are laid on graves – these flowers should never be given as a gift.

Weddings

On the day of the wedding, the bridegroom picks up his future wife from her home. The bride is dressed in a beautiful white gown, and she wears a crown and flowers in her hair. After the church ceremony, guests may shower the bride with rice – to wish her many children. She then has to cut a white ribbon that is stretched across the street by children.

After the wedding there is, of course, a big feast for family and friends. The couple drink a toast from a double-handled glass, called

Mother's Day

This day is celebrated on the last Sunday in May. But if that date is also Whit Sunday, it is celebrated on the first Sunday in June instead. On this day, children tell their mother how much she is loved and needed. They give her gifts they have made at school and a bouquet of flowers. It is also the day when Maman does not have to cook – the children either cook a nice meal for her at home or they take her out for a meal in a restaurant.

▷ *A croquembouche wedding cake* is a high cone of cream-filled buns or profiteroles. It is beautifully decorated with long caramel or chocolate threads, flowers and ribbons. The word *croquembouche* means 'crunch in the mouth'.

the *coupe de mariage*, or marriage cup. The French wedding cake is known as *croquembouche*. It is a pyramid of glazed cream-filled pastry buns. The bride and bridegroom have to try and kiss over the top of the pyramid. This symbolises a long and happy life together.

Village fêtes

In many rural areas, people used to celebrate a successful vegetable harvest by having a meal together in the village. Everyone brought their own plates and cutlery, and they also brought some food or drink along.

Nowadays, these fêtes are still celebrated in many parts of France. While people still have to bring their own cutlery, the meals have become sit-down dinners for 300 or more people. The fêtes themselves have also become larger – they often last for four days.

There are usually one or more nights of dancing. The music includes rock and pop, but also traditional French folk music, which is known as *musette* and often played on the accordion. Other regular events may include pétanque competitions, boot sales, exhibitions of art and local crafts, carriage rides, cooking competitions and traditional games.

◁ **A communal meal** at the village fête in the tiny hamlet of Les Arques in south-western France. After the meal, people dance to the music until midnight, then they stop to watch the fireworks.

MANY HAPPY RETURNS

The longest life we know of for sure was that of Jeanne Calment of France (1875–1997). She was 122 years old when she died. She was very healthy and still rode a bicycle when she was aged 100!

let's make...
DUCK BREAST

This classic dish from south-western France is a favourite meal to serve for special family occasions, such as birthdays and anniversaries. It's easy to cook and truly delicious.

WHAT YOU NEED:

SERVES 4 PEOPLE:

3 tablespoons lemon juice
2 tablespoons runny honey
salt, black pepper
2 duck breast fillets (about 300g each)
2 tablespoons cooking oil
a handful of shallots, diced

◁ Et voilà! The best duck breast ever. My sister doesn't like the skin so she leaves it on her plate. But don't skin the meat before cooking, as the skin flavours the duck.

MY TIP

You can also cook the duck in the oven. Prick the duck skin several times with a fork. Place the duck skin side down on a rack and roast it in the oven at 200°C (gas mark 6) for 20–30 minutes. Put a dish under the duck to collect the fat that runs off. Save the fat for roasting potatoes.

2 Heat the oven to 80°C.(gas mark ½). Take the fillets out of the marinade and pat them dry. Set the marinade aside.

1 In a bowl, stir together the lemon juice, honey, salt and pepper. Wash the duck breasts under cold water and pat them dry. Place them in a large ovenproof dish and rub them all over with the marinade. Cover the dish with clingfilm and chill it in the fridge for at least 2 hours.

3 In a frying pan, heat the oil over a medium heat. Place the fillets in the frying pan with the skin side down and fry them for about 7 minutes. Turn them over and fry for 5–7 minutes more.

4 **!** Put the duck breasts on a serving dish, cover and keep them warm in the oven (at 80°C or gas mark ½).

6 Slice the duck breast into thin slices and fan these out on the serving dish. Pour over a little of the sauce and serve.

5 **!** Peel and slice the shallots. Fry them in the frying pan over a medium heat until they look glassy. Pour in 5 tablespoons water. Using a wooden spoon, loosen the meat juices in the frying pan. Add the marinade. Bring the sauce to the boil and season it with salt and pepper.

let's make...
CHOCOLATE MOUSSE

Most people I know like chocolate. In fact, everyone I know likes chocolate. And this mousse is the most heavenly dessert. Unfortunately, Mum only makes it for special occasions!

WHAT YOU NEED:

SERVES 4-6 PEOPLE:

150g chocolate (milk chocolate, plain chocolate, or half of each)
2 large eggs
2 tablespoons icing sugar
125ml whipping cream or double cream
1 teaspoon vanilla extract
whipped cream and cocoa powder to serve

◁ The great thing about making chocolate mousse is that I get to lick the bowl when I'm done!

WHAT SORT OF chocolate?

You can choose any chocolate you like. Try making the mousse (which is pronounced moose) with a white chocolate or a chocolate with orange or mint flavours.

MY TIP

Melt chocolate in the microwave on medium for 1½–4 minutes until it is shiny, then stir.

1 On a chopping board, roughly chop the chocolate with a large knife. Put the chocolate into a small bowl. Now put some water into a saucepan that is slightly larger than the bowl and bring it to the boil. **!**

2 Place the bowl in the saucepan. Stir the chocolate all the time as it melts. Remove the pan from the heat.

3 Carefully separate the eggs. With a handheld whisk, beat the egg whites until stiff. Slowly sprinkle in the sugar while you whisk. Chill the stiff egg whites in the fridge. Now whisk the cream until stiff, then chill it.

4 In a large bowl, whisk the egg yolks and the vanilla extract with a clean whisk until they are creamy. Slowly stir in the melted chocolate.

5 Place the stiff cream on top of the chocolate mixture. Stir it in gently with a whisk.

6 Now place the stiff egg whites on top. Gently mix them into the mousse by pulling a spoon through both in a figure of eight. Don't mix or whisk, or the whole mousse will collapse. Chill the mousse in the fridge for at least 3 hours. Spoon it into glasses, top with whipped cream and sprinkle with some cocoa powder.

How we live in
FRANCE

Most French people live in towns, but the countryside is very important. There is a big difference between life in Paris and other large towns, and life in the 'provinces'.

City life

Parisians, and other people in French cities, work hard and are often rushed. These days, they may have a sandwich next to their computers rather than enjoying a traditional two-hour lunch break. Despite its excellent transport system, Paris experiences great traffic problems. Its ring road, called the Périphérique, is often jammed. In summer, pollution from the cars creates a cloud of smog above the larger towns.

In the city, French people are interested in fashion. Paris is one of the fashion centres of the world, and there are great fashion shops, or boutiques, in all the cities.

▽ *French beaches*, such as this one in Cassis in southern France, attract French holiday-makers as well as foreign visitors.

△ **Antiques fairs** are a national passion. Throughout the year and in every town and village, there are numerous antiques fairs, flea markets, or boot sales. Popular items to sell – and buy – are furniture, jewellery, books, old postcards, glasses and crockery.

PARDON?

Most French people speak standard French, but there are also many local dialects. Older people may sometimes be hard to understand because they speak 'patois', their rural dialect.

Holidays

Traditionally, people in France take all their holidays at the same time – the whole of the month of July or August. In the past, most people spent their holidays in France, on the coast or in the countryside. Many French families have relatives in the countryside, and some wealthier people have second homes there. Today, many people holiday abroad. They go to French islands such as Martinique, or French-speaking islands such as Mauritius. In winter, they go to North Africa or they ski in the French Alps.

If a holiday falls in the middle of the week, people often take one or two 'bridge days'. That is, they take the days in between the weekend and the holiday off too, to make a long weekend.

△ **Pétanque** is a boules game similar to crown green bowling and Italian boccia. It is played by millions of French people of all ages on holiday. The game comes from the southern port of Marseille and is now popular throughout the country.

Pastimes

The most popular sports in France are rugby and soccer, and most people support both their local and the national teams. The national teams are known as 'les bleus' (the blues) after their team colour. French sportsmen and women also excel at sailing, motor racing, judo and fencing. The varied countryside and climate allow people to ski in the Alps, to swim and sail anywhere along the coasts, and to fish, hike, explore caves and rock climb throughout the centre of the country. Not everyone is active, though. French children, like those elsewhere, also spend many hours playing computer games, watching TV and on the Internet.

Going to school

Babies and young children are cared for in day centres. After that, they go to a *maternelle*, or nursery school. They start primary school when they are six years old. There they learn reading, writing, maths, history and geography. From eleven to fourteen they go to *collège*, where they also learn two foreign languages and

▽ **The Sorbonne** is one of thirteen universities in Paris and one of the best in France. To go to university, students have to pass their *bac*. They need to get at least 10 points out of 20.

computer studies. The *lycée* is the last stage before university. It finishes with an exam known as *le bac*, the equivalent of A levels.

At lunchtime, children have a two-hour break. They go home to eat, or eat at the school *cafeteria*. Their meals may include exotic foods such as snails or octopus, as well as cheeses and desserts. There is no school on Wednesdays, but many pupils have to go to school on Saturday mornings.

State schools are secular in France, which means they are not religious. This has caused problems for Muslim girls, who are not allowed to wear their headscarves in class.

FRENCH AROUND THE WORLD

French is a main language in Bénin, Burkina Faso, Central African Republic, both Congos, Côte d'Ivoire, Gabon, Guinea, Luxembourg, Mali, Monaco, Niger, Senegal, Togo, Québec and parts of Switzerland.

let's make...
ONION SOUP

This is very much an everyday soup. Most people grow a few onions in their gardens, and every family has leftover bread that might be going stale. What better way to use it up?

WHAT YOU NEED:

SERVES 6 PEOPLE:

2 large onions
French bread, a day or two
   old and perhaps a bit stale
100g Cantal cheese,
   or Cheddar cheese
100g Swiss Gruyère
   cheese
2 tablespoons duck
   or goose fat
salt, pepper
2–2.5l water

◁ This soup is very filling. Dad says people used to eat filling starters and then only a morsel of meat. That's because meat was much more expensive.

WHAT SORT OF <u>cheese</u>?

This soup is traditionally made with two cheeses: Cantal from the Auvergne region in eastern France and Swiss Gruyère. Cantal has a strong, earthy flavour, a bit like Cheddar. You can use Cheddar instead. Gruyère is a great melting cheese. The supermarket may just call it 'Swiss cheese'.

1 Peel and finely chop the onions *(see page 5)*. Put the fat into a large saucepan and heat it over a medium heat. Add the onions. Fry and stir them over a gentle heat until they are a golden colour.

!

2 Pour about 2–2.5 litres of water into the saucepan. Season the soup generously with salt and pepper. Cover with a lid and cook the soup over a gentle heat for about 25 minutes.

!

3 Roughly grate both cheeses. Cut the bread into thin slices. Heat the oven grill.

4 Place alternate layers of bread and cheese into a deep ovenproof soup bowl. Pour the soup into the bowl, over the bread and cheese layers.

5 Place the soup bowl under the grill and grill for about 5 minutes until the cheese melts. Stir the soup with a big spoon and serve at the table.

let's make...
40-CLOVE CHICKEN

That's clove as in 'garlic clove'! We cook this dish quite often – and compete with the neighbours to see who will use the most garlic. Strangely, you can't smell it from a long way away!

WHAT YOU NEED:

SERVES 4 PERSONS:

1 large chicken
(about 1.5–2kg)
salt, black pepper
½ bunch parsley
½ bunch thyme
40 garlic cloves (or roughly
3–4 whole heads of garlic)
2 bay leaves
½ unwaxed organic lemon
4 tablespoons olive oil
250–500ml chicken stock

◁ Once the garlic is cooked you can easily pop it out of its skin. My Gran serves this dish with toasted bread, and everyone 'butters' their toast with the garlic pulp. Delicious!

How much *garlic?*

The original French recipe speaks of *quarante gousses d'ail*, which means '40 garlic cloves'. But there are other versions with only 30 cloves, and also one with two whole strings of garlic heads! The exact number doesn't really matter. Cooking makes the garlic soft and mild in flavour. Just make sure there is plenty of it!

1 Wash the chicken and pat it dry with kitchen towel. Rub it inside and out with salt and pepper. Wash the herbs and shake them dry. Peel and roughly chop four of the garlic cloves *(see page 5)*. **!**

3 Pour the oil into a large flameproof casserole. Place the chicken into the dish and turn it in the oil to coat it all over. Place the chicken breast side down.

2 Push the chopped garlic, bay leaves, parsley, half the thyme and the half lemon into the chicken. Heat the oven to 230°C (gas mark 8).

4 Wash the remaining garlic heads with their skin on. Then cut each head in half (or separate out the cloves) and place them next to the chicken. Roast chicken and garlic for 30 minutes.

5 Turn the chicken over and pour the stock into the dish. Roast for another 30–40 minutes, or until the chicken is cooked.

6 Test if the chicken is done: prick the fattest part of a leg with a skewer and pull it out again. If the juices that flow out are pink, the chicken needs to roast longer. If they are clear, it is done. Serve with the roasted garlic. **!**

let's make...
TARTE TATIN

This upside-down apple tart is totally delicious! It is served hot, straight from the oven, but it also tastes good cold. The tart can be made with other fruits, too.

WHAT YOU NEED:

MAKES 1 TARTE:

150g cold butter
150g plain flour (plus some more for the work surface)
1 pinch baking powder
2 tablespoons sugar
1 pinch salt
1 egg yolk
1kg Golden Delicious apples
170g icing sugar

PLUS:
ovenproof pie dish (about 300mm diameter)

◁ I love this tart piping hot with lots of vanilla ice cream. The contrast is delicious.

WHY IS IT CALLED: Tatin?

This tarte was invented by mistake. The Tatin sisters worked in a hotel in France. They were very busy, so they forgot to put the dough into the dish first when they were making an apple tart. But they had a great idea: they put the dough on top, cooked the tart like that, and then turned it all over. The guests loved it!

1 Cut 60g butter into cubes. Knead the butter, flour, baking powder, sugar, salt and egg yolk to a smooth dough. Shape this into a ball, wrap it in plastic wrap, and chill for 1 hour in the fridge.

2 Heat the oven to 230°C (gas mark 8). Peel the apples and cut them into quarters. Cut out the cores. Sprinkle the base of the pie dish with the icing sugar. Cook in the centre of the oven for about 10 minutes, until the sugar is a golden caramel. Add the rest of the butter to the dish and let it melt. **!**

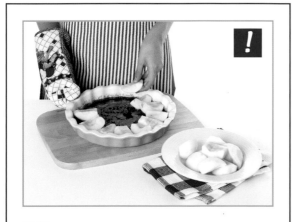

3 Arrange the apple pieces with the rounded sides down on top of the caramel. Bake for about 5 minutes in the centre of the oven.

4 Meanwhile roll out the dough on a lightly floured surface, to make a circle a little larger than the pie dish. Take the dish out of the oven and turn the heat down to 200°C (gas mark 6). **!**

5 Lift the dough on to the apples with the help of a rolling pin. Press down lightly around the edge. Prick the top several times with a fork. Bake the tarte for about 30 minutes.

6 Take the tarte out of the oven. Get your assistant to help you with this: place a large round plate on top and quickly turn both dish and plate over, holding them firmly together. Take off the pie dish and serve. **!**

Look it up
FRANCE

Armistice the end of a war; Armistice Day celebrates the end of World War I (1914–18) between the Allies and Germany on 11 November

Bastille Day the French national festival on 14 July; it celebrates the storming of the Bastille prison in Paris in 1789 and the beginning of the French Revolution

Caravane the convoy cars that advertise products ahead of the Tour de France cyclists

crêpe Suzette a sweet northern French pancake

croquembouche a French wedding cake; it is a tall pyramid of cream buns

French Revolution lasted from 1789 to 1799 and brought about major changes in French society; people rebelled because they wanted to rid themselves of a corrupt king and queen; this period ended when Napoleon came to power

gratin a dish cooked with cheese or cream that is cooked in the oven; it melts and has a crust; it often includes potatoes

méchoui a North African dish of (whole) marinated and barbecued lamb

pétanque a popular French game played with metal balls on a hard surface; the balls are thrown to be as close as possible to a smaller wooden ball, the jack

tarte tatin an upside-down cake with caramelised apples from central France; it is named after the sisters who invented it

Tour de France a French cycle race that lasts for three weeks and tours the entire country

Toussaint 1 November, or All Saints' Day; it is celebrated by visiting the graves of the family dead

Victory Day 8 May; on this day, French people celebrate freedom from German rule at the end of World War II (1939–45)

Find out more
FRANCE

Books to read

Crean, Susan
France (Discover Countries)
Wayland, 2011

Elgin, Kathy
France (World of Food)
Watts, 2010

Fisher, Teresa
France: Festivals and Food
Hodder Wayland, 2006

Hardyman, Robyn
France (Celebrate!)
Watts, 2009

Web sites to check out

**www.cia.gov/library/publications/
the-world-factbook/geos/fr.html**
The CIA's country listing on France, with
lots of facts and figures

www.www.francemag.co.uk
A site for all those who love France, with
food, drink, fashion, sports, history, art,
gardens, places to see, people gossip

**www3.nationalgeographic.com/places/
countries/country_france.html**
The National Geographic's site about
France, with information about history,
travel, flags, photographs

www.ambafrance-us.org/kids
The kids' pages of the Web site run by the
French Embassy in the United States

**www.oxfam.org.uk/coolplanet/ontheline/
explore/journey/france/frindex.htm** The
Oxfam site, with lots of facts on French
culture, cooking and scenery

Index
FRANCE